Defeating Fear, Panic, and Anxiety

A 30-day Devotional

Gwynedd Jones

First Edition 2017

Streetlamp Publishers

streetlamppublishers@gmail.com

ISBN: 978-0-9934165-2-1

Contents

Introduction

The place of experiencing fear, panic, and anxiety is often a very lonely one, as well as by its very nature extremely frightening. Some of the feelings it can bring with it are hopelessness, dread, and despair. Even getting through a single day can sometimes be a struggle. The good news however is that we are not alone, because God understands our situation. Not only does He understand what we're going through, He's already done something about it so we can be free. This 30-day devotional is aimed at helping individuals understand what God has done to help us, as well as explaining how we apply it to our lives so that we can experience the freedom we desire.

This is not a 'self-help' book, though we do have certain responsibilities if we're going to experience freedom. It's not a self-help book because we will not find the strength and resources to defeat what we're facing in and of ourselves. When we look to ourselves (our own strength, or our own will-power) to be free from fear, panic, or anxiety, it will only bring limited as well as temporary relief. The victory will never be permanent. To experience *total* victory and freedom we need to look *outside* ourselves for the power and the ability to defeat the bondage we're experiencing. Jesus has already defeated the enemy we're facing - He did it because He knew we couldn't. Because Jesus has *completely* defeated the enemy we are facing, when we look to Him to help us then the victory He has won becomes ours. He is willing to give His victory to *anybody* who asks Him. In a way, Jesus is inviting us to ride the 'coat tail' of the victory He has already won over the enemy we are facing.

Introduction

This devotional therefore looks first and foremost at how Jesus has already defeated the enemy we are facing, and then looks at how we *appropriate* that victory into our own lives.

It's important to note that this book is not limited to only helping people who are dealing with fear, panic, and anxiety. Individuals who are struggling with depression, phobias, addictions, *or any other mental oppression* will also find this book helpful because it sets out the path to freedom.

This book is not meant to be a quick fix for victory. Though we all desire to be free 'instantly', my experience has been that we move to a place of victory over time (see Deuteronomy 7:22). This daily devotional is therefore meant to be a *foundation* that equips individuals to live their lives in victory on a day-to-day basis, for the rest of their lives, which means it may need to be revisited every now and again. I first of all turned to God for help over 25 years ago, and as I read and studied the Bible I came to understand that not only did God want me to be free, He had already done something about my situation so that I *could* be free. I then applied what I saw in the Bible to my own life, and have come to experience more and more of God's goodness in setting me free. My hope is that this 30-day devotional will also help many others experience this same Goodness.

(The short italicised section at the end of each day's devotion is a prayer as well as a declaration of faith. Whenever possible, it should be spoken out aloud).

Part 1

The Old Testament Picture

'God Hears Our Cry'

*'I have surely seen the affliction of My people who are in Egypt, and
have given heed to their cry because of their taskmaster,
for I am aware of their sufferings.'*
Exodus 3:7

Fear, panic, and anxiety are enemies, and they are spiritual[1]. That is also true of every other mental affliction that tries to oppress us. Even though they exist in the 'unseen' (spiritual) realm, they are capable of wreaking havoc in people's lives in the natural realm. Because we cannot see into the spiritual realm with our natural senses, God has given us 'pictures' in the Old Testament to help us understand truths about the spiritual realm. As we read the Old Testament we are presented with a wealth of historical events; accounts of people's lives; as well as rituals and devotions that help us understand truths about the spiritual realm we would otherwise be blind to.

One such 'picture' is the account of the Israelites' bondage in Egypt (Exodus 1 & 5). The Israelites had come up into Egypt as a result of a severe famine in Canaan[2]. They settled in Egypt and their population grew so large that eventually the king of Egypt (Pharaoh) felt threatened by them[3]. That's when the Egyptians started to subject the Israelites to 'hard labour'[4] - they treated them cruelly by overworking them, making them gather their own straw to make bricks with the expectation that their production quota remained the same[5]. The Egyptians were hard and cruel taskmasters towards the Israelites, even beating them when they failed to reach their given targets[6].

This account of Israel's bondage in Egypt is a picture of the suffering a person can experience when they are subjected to fear, panic, and anxiety. Fear is able to control what the individual can or can't do; for example, some avoid lifts because they have a fear of enclosed spaces; others won't leave their house because they have a fear of open spaces. Fear, panic, and anxiety dictate how a person lives their life - they are cruel, hard taskmasters that take control of people's lives, and just like the Egyptians in this account they do not know when to stop. They will continue their cruelty without any regard for the individual.

The good news however is that in the same way God heard the cry of the Israelites and freed them from their bondage[7], He has also heard _our_ cry and has made a way for _us_ to be free from the enemy that is keeping us in bondage. In response to Israel's cry for deliverance, God sent Moses to lead them miraculously through the Red Sea. In response to _our_ cry for freedom He has sent His Son Jesus Christ who delivers us through the Cross.

Moses was simply a 'type' (or a 'picture') of the True Redeemer who was to come - Jesus Christ. Moses delivered God's people from a bondage that existed in the natural, physical realm. Jesus redeems God's people from a bondage that exists in the spiritual realm. Even though this bondage operates in the unseen realm, it is just as real, and just as devastating as the one the Israelites were subjected to. God has heard our cry and has provided a means of escape from fear, panic, and anxiety, as well as any other mental affliction that may be tormenting us.

"Father, thank You that you have heard my cry for help. Not only have You heard me, You have also sent me Your answer - Jesus Christ. Please open the eyes of my heart so I can understand what Jesus has done to set me free, and please give me the faith to receive it. I thank You Father, in Jesus' Name. Amen."

Day 2

The Enemy is Defeated

'Thus the LORD saved Israel that day from the hand of the Egyptians,
and Israel saw the Egyptians dead on the seashore'
Exodus 14:30

The next 'picture' we're looking at in the Old Testament is the account of the Israelites crossing the Red Sea. This account gives us further insight into the truths of what God has done on our behalf so we can be free from fear, panic, and anxiety. This historical event took place in the natural realm to help us understand parallel truths about the spiritual realm. The deliverance Moses brought about for the Israelites from their natural enemy (the Egyptians), helps us understand what Jesus has done to deliver us from our *spiritual* enemy of fear, panic, and anxiety.

Israel's deliverance through the Red Sea is God's response to their cry for freedom (which we looked at yesterday - Exodus 3:9). Following the ten plagues that God sent on Egypt[1], Pharaoh eventually allows the Israelites to leave but then changes his mind and gathers his army to pursue them[2]. By this time the Israelites are trapped on the edge of the Red Sea with nowhere to go, because Pharaoh and his army are now bearing down on them from the rear[3]. In a seemingly impossible situation, God does a miracle to deliver them. He tells Moses to stretch out his staff and the sea miraculously divides. The Israelites then walk through to safety on dry land[4].

The focus of today's devotion is what happens to the enemy that was pursuing them. Seeing the Israelites escaping through the Red Sea on dry land, Pharaoh and his army went in after them[5]. They soon got into difficulty because the wheels of their chariots began to come off. It was the Egyptians who now began to panic, because they realised that God was on Israel's side[6]. What happened next is highly significant. Once the Israelites were safely on the other side, Moses stretched out his staff once more and the waters now returned back to normal, destroying the enemy. Exodus 14:28 tells us that once the waters had returned, _all_ of Pharaoh's army were drowned - _'not even one of them remained'_[7]. The enemy that had subjected God's people to a cruel bondage in Egypt, the enemy that had pursued them to the utmost, had finally been _completely_ destroyed.

What Moses did in the natural realm is a picture of what Jesus has done for us spiritually. Through His death and resurrection Jesus has emphatically and completely destroyed the power of the enemy we are facing. Whether it is fear, anxiety, or panic, or any other oppression that is coming against us, Jesus has dealt with it so we can be free from our bondage. He has already done it, and it's when we look to Him that we become truly free. When we put our trust and faith in Him, we pass through the waters into our freedom. Don't allow the enemy to bully you - he is defeated, and because of your faith in Jesus, the enemy's time in your life has come to an end.

'Father, thank You that you have done what's needed to deliver me. You have dealt with my enemy in the same way You dealt with Israel's enemy thousands of years ago. I look to You for my deliverance, I put my trust in what You have done, and I thank you for hearing my cry for help. Amen.'

Drink the Living Water

'... the LORD showed him a tree, and he threw it into the waters,
and the waters became sweet'
Exodus 15:25

From the Red Sea, the Israelites travelled for three days in the wilderness until they came to a place called Marah. There was water there, but they couldn't drink it because of its bitter taste[1]. That's when the people started to grumble and complain to Moses. So God showed Moses a tree, and told him to throw it into the water. When he did, the water miraculously lost its bitterness and became sweet to the taste so they could drink it[2]. This event is an important one to look at because it has huge spiritual implications for those who put their faith in Jesus Christ.

There are a number of clues here that point to this event being a 'picture' of what Jesus has done for us through the cross and resurrection. First of all, the Israelites had just been delivered from an enemy that had been extremely brutal to them. Being released from bondage is an experience many of us can relate to when we seek help from Jesus. That was certainly my own experience, because I had been battered and plagued by bouts of fear, anxiety, and panic on a daily basis before I found my deliverance in Jesus. Secondly there is the tree, which is symbolic of the wooden cross that Jesus died on. Then thirdly, the Israelites had travelled *three days* from the Red Sea before reaching Marah. Very often when the Bible refers to a period of three days it is drawing our attention to Jesus' death and resurrection. The Holy Spirit wants to help us make the connection between what we are reading about in the Bible, with Jesus' death on the cross and His resurrection three days later. That is what is happening here - we are meant to see Jesus' death & resurrection within this event. What we have therefore at Marah is an event that happened in the natural realm, so that we can understand parallel truths regarding the spiritual realm that we cannot see.

What Moses did in the natural realm with the tree, Jesus does spiritually through the cross. Moses turned bitter water into sweet so the people could drink and be refreshed. Through His death and resurrection, Jesus has taken the 'bitter' water we were drinking before we put our faith in Him, and has given us the 'sweet' water of the Holy Spirit to refresh us. Through His death and resurrection, the bitter water of fear, anxiety, and panic (and all the other 'bitter waters' we may have been drinking) are replaced with the sweet water of peace, love, and joy from the Holy Spirit. This is why Jesus, on the last day of the Feast in Jerusalem declared that *'rivers of living water'* would flow from within the person who believes in Him (see John 7:37-39). That is great news because it means that if our faith is in Jesus Christ, we who were once held in captivity and were drinking 'bitter water', now have the living water of the Holy Spirit within us!

'Father, thank you that because of what Jesus has done through His death and resurrection, you have made the living water of the Holy Spirit available to me. Thank you that the Holy Spirit is within me, and I pray You would teach me how to allow this living water to flow like a river from within me so I can be filled with Your love, joy, and peace. Amen'

The LORD Our Healer

'... I, the LORD, am your healer'
Exodus 15:26

There is another important lesson we can learn from this event at Marah where the bitter water was turned sweet[1]. It is here at Marah that God reveals one of His names - *'Jehovah Rapha'* - which means *'I, the LORD am your healer'*[2].

No one name can fully describe the nature of God, because God has many 'facets' to His character. He is Loving, He is Righteous, He is Compassionate and He is Kind. He is Peace, He is Faithful, He is Almighty - the list of His excellent qualities is endless. No one single name can therefore encompass nor describe all He is. This is why God chose to reveal Himself in the Bible through various names, each name describing an important attribute and aspect of His character. It is here at Marah that He reveals His nature as Healer - *'I, the LORD, am your healer'*[2].

It is significant that this name *'Jehovah Rapha'* is the first name He reveals to His people following their deliverance from Egypt. It is not accidental - God deliberately chose to reveal this Name first. God wanted His people to know that He is the One who would heal them of the physical, emotional, and psychological scars resulting from their bondage in Egypt. Effectively, God was saying to them - *'whatever scars, whatever hurts you are carrying from your time in Egypt, I am your healer. If your bodies need healing after the beating you took, if you are diseased because of a poor diet, I will heal you. If you have been mentally or emotionally scarred by your cruel experience, I am your healer. In whatever area of your life you need healing - I am your healer'*. This was the urgent truth God wanted His people to know, which is why He chose this name as the first name He reveals to Israel following their deliverance.

God does not change³, and He is saying exactly the same thing to us today. Through faith in Jesus Christ, we are delivered from our captivity. God wants us to know as an urgent truth that whatever scars we may be carrying from the life we had before placing our faith in Him, He will heal us. God is saying to all who put their faith in His Son Jesus - *'whatever hurts you are carrying from the life you had before coming to know Me, I will heal you. Whether they are physical, psychological, or emotional, I will heal you. If you are struggling with fears, phobias, panic attacks, or any other oppression, I will heal you'*.

Whatever area of your life needs healing - come to Him who is Healer. It may be that you are struggling with your emotions, with an addiction, or with a phobia; or it may be a mental or physical illness that you need God to help you with. Whatever it is, ask Him not only to help you, but also to heal you. You may have already come to the cross of Jesus and received Him, come again because there is no limit to His grace. If you need to come for the first time, don't let anything stop you. He is the LORD who heals. There is no reason to delay.

"Father, thank You for revealing to me that You are my Healer. Thank You Lord that You are able to heal every area of my life that is broken. Help me to walk into the healing You desire for me to have. I give You thanks and praise Lord for what You are doing in my life. In Jesus' Name. Amen"

Driving out the Enemy

'... then you shall drive out all the inhabitants of the land from before you...
for I have given the land to you to possess it.'
Numbers 33:52-53

God heard the cry of His people when they were in captivity.
He provided a miraculous delivery through the Red Sea, and in
the process completely destroyed the enemy who had kept
them in bondage. At Marah He provided sweet water to refresh
them, and declared He was their Healer. Was that it for them
now? Had the time come for them to sit back with their feet up
and start relaxing? Not really. God's plan wasn't for them to
settle in the wilderness but rather to occupy a far better place, a
place beyond the River Jordan. It was Canaan they needed to
head for, because it was here that God had promised to meet all
their needs[1].

Up until now, God had done all the fighting on their behalf; all
they needed to do was follow. He had deliberately chosen a
route out of Egypt to avoid the need for them to fight, because
He knew they would have buckled under the pressure[2]. Things
change now however, because God starts telling them they will
need to stand up to their enemies and do battle against them.
But He didn't expect them to do it in their own strength - He
repeatedly tells them He had already gone before them, and
had already dealt with their enemies[3]. Their part is to possess
what He's already provided for them[4]. In addition, He tells
them this was not going to be an overnight victory[5] - there were

going to be battles ahead but as long as they kept their focus on Him, He promised success and victory[6].

God explained to them they would need to *'drive out'* the present occupiers of the land He was giving them[7]. It's important to see the spiritual equivalent of this. Spiritually, God has a place for us where we experience His love, peace, and joy in the deepest part of our being. The Bible calls this place God's 'Sabbath rest'[8]. That's where He wants to take us (spiritually not geographically), and provided we will keep our focus on Him we will get there. But the problem in the meantime is that there are other tenants occupying this place. Those occupants may be fear, anxiety, or panic. In fact the present occupiers can be anything that is in opposition to the peace, love, joy, and righteousness that God wants us to have. This is why we need to engage in a fight - we need to *drive out* these unwanted tenants so that God's promises of love, peace, joy, righteousness, security etc. can take their place in order for us to enter into God's Sabbath rest.

God is not asking us to do this by ourselves, nor in our own strength. We're not even being asked to fight a battle that hasn't already been won! He has already won the war 2000 years ago, which is why those who have faith in Christ are already conquerors[9] - but we need to trust in *His* victory and *His* strength, not our own. Tell God today that you are willing to fight the *'good fight of faith'*[10] so you can drive out your spiritual enemies, acknowledging also you can't do it in your own strength but are looking to Him to help you.

"Father, You are good to me. You want me to be free and You want me to enjoy my life. I acknowledge today Lord that I need to fight this enemy that is stealing the peace, the joy, and the love You want me to experience in You. I make a decision today Lord to stand up to fight this enemy, acknowledging I can only do it in Your strength. I trust in Your faithfulness Lord. In Jesus' Name. Amen."

Day 6

The Enemy is Terrified of Us

'... their hearts melted, and there was no spirit in them any longer because of the sons of Israel.'
Joshua 5:1

The last picture we will look at from the Old Testament is the account of Rahab in Joshua chapter 2. In this account, the Israelites were on the verge of invading the land God had promised them. Joshua was now Israel's leader and he sent two men across the river Jordan to spy out the land. A woman named Rahab gave refuge to the two spies in her house in Jericho, hiding them from the king who was searching for them (see Joshua 2).

During the dialogue Rahab had with the spies[1], she reveals some details that were a great encouragement to them. This is what Rahab said:

"I know that the Lord has given Israel this land. Everyone shakes with fear because of you. We heard how the Lord dried up the Red Sea so you could leave Egypt. And we heard how you destroyed Sihon and Og, those two Amorite kings east of the Jordan River. We know that the Lord your God rules heaven and earth, and we've lost our courage and our will to fight."
(Joshua 2:9-11 CEV).

What Rahab revealed was how Israel's enemy was thinking and how they felt. The spies now knew that the enemy they had been told to *'drive out'* was absolutely terrified of them. The enemy had heard the reports of what God had already done on Israel's behalf and it made them tremble with fear. Knowing their enemy lacked the courage to fight because they were terrified of them gave the Israelites a huge psychological advantage[2].

God has given us this picture to help us understand the same truths apply to us from a spiritual perspective. Israel had a *physical* enemy that was terrified of them; we have a *spiritual* enemy who is terrified of us. Israel's enemies were terrified because they had come to understand God was on Israel's side. Because He is God Almighty, they realised trying to fight the Israelites was a lost cause because effectively they would be fighting against God[3]. It is the same for us - our spiritual enemy (fear, panic, or any other oppression) know they cannot defeat us because they know God is on our side[4]. Make a decision today that you are going to submit yourself to God and that you're going to stand up to your enemy in God's strength. If you do, it's only a matter of time before he flees[5].

'Thank You Father that you have gone ahead of me and dealt with my enemies of fear, panic, and anxiety (also include here any other spiritual enemies you may be aware of). Thank you that because You are my God, my enemies are now terrified of me. As long as I stay in You, they know they will not be able to defeat me. Please continue to give me the courage and the strength I need to drive out these enemies from my life, so I can fully enter into the love, peace, and joy that You want me to experience. I pray this in Jesus' Name. Amen'

Part 2

What Jesus Has Done

God Has Kept His Promise

*"So I have come down to deliver them from the power of the Egyptians,
and to bring them up from that land to a good and spacious land'*
Exodus 3:8

We started on Day 1 by looking at how God heard the people's cry for help so they could be set free from their bondage in Egypt (Exodus 3:7). In the verse that immediately follows (Exodus 3:8 above), God declares that He has *come down* to deliver them from this cruel captivity. From the outset, God was making His intention known - He would not be orchestrating things from a distance, but rather He would 'come down' from His heavenly throne and take a personal involvement in the deliverance of His people.

That's why Jesus came. God, who is Spirit[1], entered into our physical realm as a man. That man is Jesus. At His birth, Jesus was declared 'Immanuel' – which means 'God with us'[2]. Through the prophets, God made it clear there was only ONE Saviour – and that He Himself was that Saviour[3]. With the birth of Jesus, the Saviour who dwelt in the spiritual realm now entered the physical realm, with the angel proclaiming to the shepherds His arrival[4]. God has kept His promise to come down to deliver His people, and we will see over the next couple of weeks how Jesus is the fulfilment of God's promise of deliverance[5].

Psalm 107:20 tells us God *'sent His word and healed them, and delivered them from their destructions.'* God has kept this promise by sending Jesus, because Jesus is the 'Word' the psalmist is referring to[6]. This 'Word' became flesh when Jesus was born[7]. Not only did Jesus fulfil *this* promise from the Word of God, He fulfilled them all[8]. We can see from this verse in Psalm 107 that Jesus came to fulfil God's promise to heal us, and also to deliver us from our 'destructions'. My personal experience is that fear, panic, and anxiety are destructive forces that try to ruin our lives, so for me they come under this category of 'destructions'. I would expect others can also relate to this from their own personal experience. What this verse tells us however is that God has sent Jesus (His Word) so we can be delivered from these damaging forces! When we come to Jesus, we can be set free from the things that are trying to ruin us! This is wonderful news for anybody and everybody who is struggling with fear, anxiety, or panic, or any other oppression that is trying to destroy our lives.

We are not alone in our battle against the fear that is trying to come against us. God is a God of His Word, so He has come down to help us. He took on 'flesh and blood' in order to deal with the enemy that is harassing us[9]. He was willing to suffer so we could be set free[10]. Our responsibility is to make sure we take advantage of this amazing grace that has been provided for us. How do we do that? Simply by believing in the One whom God has sent[11]. Schedule some quality time today to meditate on this gift that God has given us – His Son Jesus – and thank Him for coming to set you free.

'Thank You Lord that You chose to be personally involved in my deliverance from fear, anxiety, and panic. Thank You that You did not choose to send a representative, but that You Yourself came to this earth as a man so You could set me free. You are the One who personally suffered on that cross so I could be free. I am so grateful to you, please help me follow You and learn from You so that I can experience the freedom You have won for me. I pray this in Jesus' Name. Amen'

Jesus Came As Our Ransom

"The Son of Man did not come to be served, but to serve,
and to give His life a ransom for many"
Matthew 20:28

Moses delivered Israel from their slavery in Egypt through the Red Sea. Jesus delivers us from the slavery of sin through His cross and resurrection. One is physical; the other is spiritual.

Slavery is cruel, and it is evil. Slavery means a person loses their free will and comes under the influence and control of another. A slave loses their freedom to make choices that prosper them as individuals, as well as their family. Slaves are treated as a commodity, not as individuals who are precious in the sight of God. This is what has happened in the world for centuries, and it continues today.

The slavery that sin brings is no less destructive to an individual, except it is happening in the spiritual realm not the physical. It still controls the individual's life, it still steals their free will, it still dominates their life, and its destructive force spreads to affect the wider family also. Jesus however came to save us from this cruel bondage.

By definition, a slave has neither the authority, nor the power to free him or herself. The individual is under the authority of their master – being told where to go and what to do, and it is the same with sin. The only way a natural slave could be freed was either for their master to release them voluntarily, or someone else would pay a redemption price resulting in a change of ownership. Some slaves were treated so cruelly they decided to run away from their captor. That is not freedom because they would constantly be living in fear knowing they were being hunted down and would eventually be killed.

Satan would never voluntarily release those he keeps captive to sin; we know that from the account of Pharaoh - pursuing the Israelites even to the very last. The only option left to us therefore is for someone to 'buy' us out of slavery. That's what Jesus has done! Jesus gave *Himself* as the Ransom to set us free[1]. He has paid the *redemption price* that was required for us to undergo a change of ownership with His own life. He is the *only* redemption price that can pay for our freedom - there is no other way[2]. Looking to any other 'source' for a complete and total deliverance from sin will be unfruitful.

When we make a choice to put our faith in Jesus, what we're actually doing is making a declaration to the spiritual realm that we are choosing a new Master for our lives[3]. This Master whom we are surrendering our lives to has a good plan for our lives[4], and wants to take us into wholeness[5]. Wholeness simply means to prosper in every area of our lives - in our health, relationships, security, peace, finances, purpose etc. That's the place where we will enjoy the abundant life Jesus came to give us[6]. Jesus is the key to this abundant life; it is the place where we are free from the tyranny of fear, anxiety, and panic. Take time today to think about the price Jesus has paid to set you free, and thank Him for it.

"Father, thank You for paying the price to redeem me from the slavery to sin. It cost You Your life to buy me from that slavery. I acknowledge before You that You are the only Ransom payment that is good enough to set me free. I choose to surrender to You Lord Jesus, and believe that You have a good plan for my life to see me prosper in every area. In Jesus' Name. Amen."

Jesus Has Broken the Power of Sin

*"For He rescued us from the domain of darkness, and transferred
us to the kingdom of His beloved Son"*
Colossians 1:13

This verse tells us we have been rescued from the 'domain' of darkness. The definition of domain is *'an area of territory owned or controlled by a particular ruler or government'*. In the New Testament, the Greek word translated here as 'domain' is more frequently translated *power*, as well as *authority* (*'exousia'*). So to be in someone's *domain* means we are subject to the one who rules the domain; it means they have power over us; we are under their authority as well as being subject to their control and influence over us. It is our sin that takes us into the domain of darkness[1] and as we saw yesterday, we are helpless to release ourselves.

Jesus came so we could choose another 'domain' - another kingdom. When we choose Him, the authority, the power, and the control that the domain of darkness has over us is broken. That's because Jesus has a *greater* power and a *greater* authority than satan[2]. Jesus exercises His greater power and authority on our behalf when we choose to put our faith in Him. Jesus demonstrated His superior power and authority all through His earthly ministry when He drove out the kingdom of darkness from people's lives so the Kingdom of God could come in[3]. If we have surrendered our lives to Jesus and our faith is in Him, then we have *already* transferred kingdoms[4]. We are no longer in satan's 'dominion'; we are now in the Kingdom of God's 'beloved Son' - the kingdom of Jesus.

Because we are no longer in satan's domain, we are no longer under his control and influence, he has lost his authority over us. Jesus has taken us out of that kingdom and into a new Kingdom. Satan no longer has control over us unless we choose to allow him. Faith in Jesus means we have crossed the border from a spiritually wicked and evil kingdom, into a kingdom where we will thrive and prosper[5].

Because this happens at a spiritual level, there is a danger we can miss the reality and truth of it. There is a danger of understanding this principle and agreeing with it on an intellectual level, without it actually sinking into our hearts so it can make a difference in our lives. Once we allow the truth that we have been transferred out of satan's dominion to settle in our *hearts*, a change will happen within us. We will find a confidence and boldness starting to rise from within. We will begin to see how we do not have to allow fear, panic, and anxiety to dominate us any longer because they have no authority over us - Jesus has paid (with His life) for us to be free from them.

This is not a theory, nor a philosophy, nor wishful thinking - this is a truth and a reality. The Bible tells us when our faith is in Jesus Christ we are no longer under the authority, nor the dominion, nor the control of sin (kingdom of darkness). We have a new King sitting on the throne of our hearts, a King who has paid the price for us to be free[6]. That is worth celebrating!

"Father, thank You that You have transferred me from the authority, from the influence, and from the dominion of darkness. It no longer has control over my life because I have made Jesus Lord. He is the One whom I choose as King to sit on the throne of my heart, and no one else. My prayer to You today Father is for the truth that I am in Your Kingdom to penetrate my heart so deeply that I will have the boldness and the confidence to stand up against any other 'power' that may try to control me. I ask this in Jesus' Name. Amen."

Jesus Has Destroyed the Works of the Devil

"The Son of God appeared for this purpose, to destroy the works of the devil"
1 John 3:8b

Jesus had an assignment. He had a purpose for coming into the earthly realm. We can see what the assignment was from the verse above - Jesus came to *'destroy the works of the devil'*. In the process of fulfilling this assignment, Jesus also accomplishes a number of other things. He demonstrated how the power and authority of the Kingdom of God is superior to that of the kingdom of darkness. Jesus was also successful at revealing the Father's heart to the world - a heart of love, compassion, mercy, and grace. Jesus also defeated death, and through His own death and resurrection He has opened up the way for us to know the One who is Life. For today however, we're keeping our focus on Jesus' assignment to *'destroy the works of the devil'*.

So, what are the works of the devil that Jesus came to destroy - what do they look like? The simplest way to answer that question is to look at what Jesus did during His earthly ministry. Jesus' ministry was packed full of supernatural works. He brought miraculous healing to people[1], He set people free by casting out demons[2], and He fed thousands of people at one 'sitting' despite having the most meagre of provisions[3]. He also brought forgiveness and mercy to people who deserved the death sentence because they were guilty of breaking God's Law[4]. In Acts 10:38 we are told how God anointed Jesus with the Holy Spirit and with power. The result of this anointing was *'He went about doing good and healing all who were oppressed by the devil'*. Jesus was able to go about 'doing good' because God had anointed Him for that purpose. The manifestation of that 'goodness' was healing people of sickness and disease; it included setting people free from spiritual bondage; as well as showing mercy and forgiveness to those who were guilty. The reason Jesus *needed* to go about 'doing good' was because of, and in response to, the oppression the devil had brought upon the people Jesus ministered to.

Before Jesus 'did good' to them, the devil had oppressed these people with sickness, with spiritual bondage, with guilt and shame etc. Jesus destroyed these works of the devil by bringing healing, deliverance, mercy and forgiveness. Jesus had the power and the authority to crush what the devil had brought into these people's lives, and then restore them to how God wanted them to be - healed, free, and made whole.

Jesus is the same now as He was then[5]. In the same way He healed people from sickness and disease then, He does it today. In the same way He brought forgiveness to those who suffered guilt and shame, He does it today. In the same way He delivered people from spiritual oppression, He does it today. The fear, panic, and anxiety - or any other oppression you may be experiencing - is no match for Jesus. Jesus was given an assignment - to destroy the works of the devil, and when we look at the bigger picture of His earthly ministry it is safe to say 'Mission Accomplished'[6]. Jesus was successful in His mission to destroy the works of the devil, and He continues to do so today in the lives of those who put their faith and trust in Him.

"Thank You Father for sending Jesus on an assignment to destroy the works of the devil. I can see from your Word how Jesus brought Your goodness into people's lives by destroying what the devil had brought. Father I put my trust in You that the fear, the anxiety, and the panic that is trying to come against me are destroyed because You are with me. I trust You Lord, and thank You for Your goodness in setting me free. In Jesus' Name. Amen."

Jesus Has Disarmed the Enemy

"When He had disarmed the rulers and authorities, He made a public display of them, having triumphed over them through Him"
Colossians 2:15

The 'rulers and authorities' referred to in this verse are *the powers and the spiritual forces of wickedness* that exist in the spiritual realm[1]. They are the very forces that are trying to come against us through fear, panic, and anxiety. They are not from God, because God has not given us a spirit of fear, nor of bondage[2].

This is a verse I personally go back to whenever I sense fear and anxiety trying to come against me. I go to this verse to remind myself of what God has done to the enemy that is trying to intimidate me. What I'm feeling is real, so I take myself to a quiet place and then remind myself of the truth of what Jesus has done on the cross regarding the fear that is rising inside of me.

Because of the sacrifice of Jesus on the cross, satan has been 'disarmed'. When someone is disarmed, it means they have been stripped of their armaments. The weapons they once used to fight with have been taken from them. Not only do they not have any weapons to fight with, they don't have any weapons to defend themselves with either. They are in an extremely vulnerable position and are at the mercy of the one they are fighting against. Most of us have probably seen film footage from the Second World War where thousands of enemy soldiers are being led away with nothing but the clothes they were wearing. For them, the fight is over - they have no weapons to fight with and are resigned to defeat. What is also striking about these images is that it takes only a relatively few soldiers who are *armed*, to surround and control *thousands* of soldiers who are unarmed. That's the power of having, or not having a weapon.

One of the most powerful weapons satan has is *deception*. He deceives people because he is a liar and the father of lies[3]. There is a simple antidote to deception - truth. Once we come into truth about a matter, a lie or a deception cannot stand - it is disarmed. Jesus is the Truth[4]; as is the Word of God[5] so when we put our faith in Jesus and what His Word says, satan is disarmed because his lies cannot stand. When he tries to bring fears and worries about our health, about our relationships, about our finances, if we go into the Word of God and search out what the TRUTH is saying and then put our faith in it - satan is immediately disarmed. His lies cannot stand against the truth of God's Word, and he will flee[6]. So today, if fear or anxiety regarding a particular situation in your life tries to rise up within you, go to the Word of God and *counter* that attack with the Truth of the Word. See what God says about your situation, and do not listen to the lies the devil is trying to tell you. Then settle it in your heart that it's the Word you're going to believe - no matter what the circumstances look like.

"Father, thank You for Your Word. Jesus says Your Word is truth, and I believe Him. I ask You Father to help me get Your Word so deeply embedded into my heart, that when the enemy brings fears by telling me lies, it will be like water off a duck's back, because Your truth has set me free. In Jesus' Name I pray. Amen."

Day 12

Jesus Made a Public Exhibit of the Enemy

"When He had disarmed the rulers and authorities, He made a public
display of them, having triumphed over them through Him"
Colossians 2:15

The second truth we can draw from this verse in Colossians is how Jesus, through His cross, made a *'public display'* of the defeat God has inflicted on satan. Through the cross of Jesus Christ, God has given the world clear proof of how He has destroyed the devilish forces of wickedness that exist in the spiritual realm. These wicked forces include fear, panic, and anxiety, as well as any other oppressive spirit that may be trying to come against us.

In one way the cross is very beautiful, yet in another way it is extremely ugly. The cross is beautiful because it demonstrates the amazing love and mercy of God. It shows how God entered the physical realm as a man[1] and then gave Himself to die as a sacrifice for our sin[2]. He took *our* guilt, *our* shame, *our* sickness, and *our* punishment upon Himself and paid the price with His own life so we could be free[3]. Only the love, mercy, and grace of God can do this and it is clearly demonstrated through the cross of Jesus Christ[4]. Yet on the other hand the cross is very ugly because it is a display of sin. Jesus was 'made sin on our behalf'[5]; so what we see on the cross is what sin looks like when it is allowed a free reign on a person's body. Jesus' body was so distorted and disfigured as a result of sin that He was unrecognisable[6].

29

It was Jesus' body that hung on the cross, but it was no longer the perfectly healthy body that was once His. His body had now been 'made sin' because it had been beaten, it had been whipped, and it was now bearing the world's sicknesses[7]. Jesus' body had once been a holy and righteous temple for God's Spirit[8]; it wasn't this perfect body that now hung on the cross because Jesus' body had been 'made sin' on our behalf. Sin and death is a spirit[9] and because Jesus had been 'made sin for us'[5], the body hanging on the cross was now the incarnation of that spirit of sin and death. As this body of sin died on the cross, God was making a public statement, He was making a declaration for all to see that sin was being dealt with once and for all and was being put to death. What was happening to Jesus' body on the cross was the reflection of what was happening in the unseen realm - the spiritual forces of wickedness were being destroyed, defeated, and being put to death.

If our faith is in Jesus Christ then the fear, the panic, and the anxiety that try to oppress us have been defeated and destroyed through the cross. The body of sin that died on the cross is the clear proof of how God has destroyed the spirit of sin and death that is behind these oppressions. God doesn't want it kept a secret - which is why Jesus being made sin was on public display for all to see.

"Father, You paid the ultimate price for me to be free from the spirit of sin and death that would try to enslave me. I thank You that You gave Your own life, and You suffered in the most cruel and inhumane way so I could be free. Thank You Father that as I look at the cross I see Your great love for me in the price You paid, but I also see the truth of how you put sin to death. When fear, anxiety, or panic try to intimidate me, please help me remember what You have done and the price You have paid on the cross. You have made a public display of the defeat You have inflicted on my enemy. I thank You Father and praise You in Jesus' Name. Amen."

Jesus Has Triumphed Over the Enemy

"When He had disarmed the rulers and authorities, He made a public display of them, having triumphed over them through Him"
Colossians 2:15

There is one more truth we need to look at from this verse that will help us in our fight against spiritual oppression. We've already seen how the enemy has been disarmed and made a public spectacle of; today we will look at how this verse shows us the enemy is no longer a threat to us because of the cross of Jesus Christ.

When Roman Generals were successful in conquering a new province or territory, they would bring the conquered king or monarch of that province back to Rome and then parade them through the city. This parade was a huge occasion and crowds would line the streets so they could witness the event. The manner in which the defeated enemy was paraded is very significant.

The defeated king or ruler would have their thumbs cut off, as well as their big toes. They would then be dragged naked through the streets tied to a chariot. Their thumbs were cut off so they could no longer use a sword to fight with. Having no big toe meant they were unable to ride a horse because they couldn't manage the stirrups to control the mount. Both these things were meant to send a message to the Roman citizens witnessing the parade that this enemy was no longer a threat to them. Being stripped naked and dragged behind a chariot would further reinforce this - the once regally dressed monarch had fallen from their throne and was now fully under the control of the Roman military machine. Though cruel, it was a powerfully symbolic statement that gave every Roman citizen the confidence and security of being part of an Empire that was so powerful it could not be matched militarily.

The Greek word Paul uses in this verse for 'triumphed over' is the same Greek word that was used to describe this parade through Rome. Paul wants us to understand that in the same way the conquered enemies of Rome were no longer a threat to the Roman Empire; satan is no longer a threat to those who are citizens of God's Kingdom. Take a few moments now and imagine you are part of the crowd watching the procession through Rome. What would you see, and how does that encourage you regarding what Jesus has done to your spiritual enemy?

"Father, thank You for what You have done through the cross of Jesus Christ. Thank You for the truth that the enemy coming against me has been disarmed, made an exhibit of, and has been triumphed over. The cross of Jesus Christ shows me Your total and absolute Victory over satan, a defeat from which he cannot recover. Help me Lord to receive and know that truth in my heart so I can stand up in the strength and boldness You give me. In Jesus' Name. Amen."

Jesus Came to Reveal the Father's Heart

"He who sees Me sees the One who sent Me."
John 12:45

The religious leaders in Jesus' day had an image of God that was wrong. That's why they clashed with Jesus. Their image of God was someone who was quick to judge people, someone who would mete out a severe punishment because He was a stickler for rules. When Jesus came on the scene to show what God was *really* like, they didn't like it because it cut across everything they believed in and had built their lives upon. They hated Jesus for it, which is why they plotted to kill Him[1].

Jesus came to show the compassionate heart of God. He came to show how God is a loving Father. He came to show the world what God is *really* like – not what people *think* He is like. Jesus is qualified to show what God is like because He is the *image* of the One who exists in the spiritual realm[2]. Because He *exactly* represents God[3], when we look at Jesus' earthly ministry we're not left guessing what God is like. If for some reason we have an image of God that does not line up with what we see in Jesus, we need to seriously question what we believe because in Jesus we see a true, accurate, and exact representation of God.

Jesus didn't do anything He didn't see His Father doing[4], nor did He say anything He hadn't heard His Father say[5]. So when Jesus showed compassion, mercy, and forgiveness, He was simply reflecting what he'd seen and heard His Father do. God had taken on flesh and blood[6] and had come to tabernacle ('pitch His tent') amongst people on the earth[7]. He hadn't come to remain detached from people's pain and suffering, He was now right there in the middle of it, getting His hands dirty as He touched lepers and laid hands on all sorts of sick people[8]. God's heart was stirred with such compassion when He saw people bound by either sickness or oppression it moved Him to His very core[9]. The Heart of the One who existed in the spiritual realm was now being revealed to the world through the life and ministry of Jesus Christ[10].

Before Jesus came, it wasn't possible to know God as a Father. It wasn't possible to have an intimate, personal relationship with God because sin prevented it, and sin hadn't been dealt with fully until Jesus came. Once Jesus dealt with sin however, it opened up the door for God to come into an individual's heart and know Him as Father, if they so desired[11]. That's what Jesus made possible, and our privilege is that we can now know the Father in the same intimate way that Jesus did[12]. This is the most precious gift any human being can receive, and it's what we've been created for. We need to make sure we take hold of it with all of our heart.

"Father, there is so much I want to thank You for. Thank You for adopting me into Your family. Thank You that You have made it possible for me to know You as my Heavenly Father. Thank You for getting involved in my situation. Thank You that You will never leave me, even during those times I let You down because our relationship is based on Your love, not my performance. You are my most precious possession as well as my greatest treasure Father, and I thank You in Jesus' Name. Amen."

Day 15

Jesus Came to Restore Our Authority

".... those who receive the abundance of grace and of the gift of righteousness will reign in life through the One, Jesus Christ."
Romans 5:17b

God created man in His own image and gave him authority to rule the earth[1]. Rather than being obedient to God's instruction not to eat of the tree of the knowledge of good and evil[2], Adam and Eve believed what the serpent said and as a result they became subjects in the kingdom of darkness[3]. From a position of having a God-given authority to rule the earth, they now found themselves subject to the one who rules the kingdom of darkness. They had effectively handed over their authority to satan and there was nothing they could do about it.

Because God had given the authority to rule the earth to *man*, He couldn't intervene. His hands were tied so to speak, because even though God is sovereign, one thing He cannot do is go back on His Word. He wasn't now able to call 'time out' and pull back what He had given[4]. The authority had been given to man, and therefore only man could take it back. The problem was however that not only were Adam and Eve subject to the kingdom of darkness, every other person born since is also subject to it (except Jesus). This is because every person born 'naturally' carries the fallen nature of Adam[5], which is the reason we need to be born-again to enter the Kingdom of God[6].

Jesus came as a man so that as a man He could take back the authority which had been lost. Because Jesus was born of the

35

Holy Spirit[7], He was not a subject in the kingdom of darkness. He was not born of the fallen nature of Adam so the spirit of sin and death had no authority over Him - Jesus was born of the Spirit of God. Jesus was the only man born outside the jurisdiction of satan. When Jesus died on the cross it wasn't because His life had been taken from Him, it was because He had freely chosen to *offer* Himself on our behalf. He *allowed* the spirit of sin and death to take Him so that three days later it would be defeated through His resurrection[8].

Jesus is victorious over satan and as with any victorious king, Jesus took the spoils of war. This included man's authority to rule the earth that was lost at the Fall. Jesus then gave that authority back to man[9]. In *His* authority, Jesus wants us to push back the darkness that is not only trying to come against us personally, but also the darkness that is trying to invade our families, our communities, as well as our country. Today, start seeing yourself as the *'head not the tail'* and as the one who is *'above not underneath'*. This is in line with God's promise that is now fulfilled in Jesus Christ[10].

"Father, thank You that the Gospel is such good news. Your Word tells me that I am no longer a subject in the kingdom of darkness, but it also tells me that I am now the one in authority. This is because You have given me Your authority when I put my faith in Jesus. Help me get this truth deep down into my heart so that I can start to push back the darkness I'm experiencing in my life. I ask this in Jesus' Name. Amen."

Jesus Came to Make Us Whole

"He bore the punishment that made us whole; by His wounds we are healed"

Isaiah 53:5 (CEB)

Throughout the Old Testament, God consistently promised salvation to His people[1]. The word used in the Hebrew for *salvation* has a broad meaning that includes deliverance from *anything and everything* that God's people needed saving from - war, enemies, sickness, distress etc. At His birth Jesus was declared the Saviour who would bring this promised salvation[2].

The earthly ministry of Jesus is the outworking of this salvation. The healing Jesus brought is the freedom from the enemy of sickness and disease[3]. The deliverance Jesus brought is freedom from the enemy of spiritual oppression[4]. The forgiveness Jesus brought is the release from guilt, shame, and condemnation[5]. Whatever was oppressing people - whether it was physical or spiritual, Jesus brought God's salvation to them and set them free.

God wants to do more than heal us. He wants to do more than deliver us from oppression. He wants to do more than forgive our sins. God wants us to experience *wholeness*. Being made whole means every area of our lives prospers. It means we are physically, psychologically, as well as emotionally healthy. It means we are secure in God's love and know His will for our lives. It means we are prospering financially as well as in our relationships. No area of our lives is untouched when we experience wholeness. The Hebrew word that describes this Biblical 'wholeness' is *shalowm*. This word is often translated 'peace', and though correct it does not fully convey the depth of what God wants us to have in promising *shalowm* to His people. *Shalowm* means there is nothing broken, nothing missing in our lives because we are whole in every area.

Jesus has paid the ultimate price for us to have this *shalowm* of God. When we look at the verse above from Isaiah 53:5 we can see how He took upon Himself the punishment that would bring us wholeness. He took a beating to His physical body that included being whipped[6]. He was spat on, and slapped across the face[7]. He took nails in His hands and feet on the cross[8]. He took all of this punishment so that we could have wholeness. This is why He declared *'I came that they may have life, and have it abundantly'* (see John 10:10).

The wholeness that Jesus has paid the price for us to have includes freedom from fear, panic, and anxiety. It includes deliverance from any and every spiritual oppression that may be trying to come against us. It includes deliverance from guilt, shame, and condemnation. It is freedom from lack and insecurity. As you spend time today meditating on God's promise of wholeness to you, identify the areas of your life where you want to be restored, and then take them to God in prayer.

"Father, thank You that You have a concern about every area of my life. Thank You that through the cross of Jesus You have dealt with everything so that I can live a healthy, prosperous, and purposeful life. You have every base covered in my life, and I ask You to help me walk into the fullness of what You have won for me through the cross. In Jesus' Name I pray. Amen."

Day 17

Jesus Has Broken the Power of the Devil

"Because God's children are human beings - made of flesh and blood - the Son also became flesh and blood. For only as a human being could he die, and only by dying could he break the power of the devil....."
Hebrews 2:14 (NLT)

The devil's power has been broken - this is what the verse above is telling us. The original Greek word used in this verse points to the devil having been *'rendered entirely useless; abolished; destroyed, done away with; made of no effect; made void; brought to nought'*[1]. These are powerful descriptions of what has happened to the devil when God took on flesh and blood and then died on the cross for us.

Our day-to-day experience however may not reflect what this verse is telling us regarding the state of our enemy. We may be able to agree with the verse in our heads, but the reality of our *experience* is telling us something completely different. Often, our *experience* doesn't bear witness to the devil having been *'rendered entirely useless'*, nor *'abolished'*, because we're still experiencing a real, and often merciless oppression coming against us through fear and anxiety. So what is going on? Why are we still experiencing spiritual oppression when the Bible clearly tells us the power of the enemy has been destroyed?

It is true that Jesus has completely defeated our spiritual enemy. The outworking of that victory in a person's life however does not happen automatically. How effective Jesus' victory becomes in a person's life is down to the individual. That's because as individuals we have a responsibility to *appropriate* what Jesus has done into our own lives, at a personal level. Jesus' victory over the devil will not simply drop into our laps; we have to draw it *by faith* for it to make a difference.

Jesus has won the war. He is victorious, and He gives His victory to everyone who puts their faith in Him. The individual then has a responsibility to *take*, to *apply*, as well as to *appropriate* that victory into his or her own life in order to walk into the *experience* of the freedom Jesus has won for them. Its when we don't know how to appropriate Jesus' victory for ourselves that we remain frustrated and disheartened, because on one hand we're seeing a true and genuine hope in the Word of God, yet on the other we're not experiencing it.

Part 3 is all about our responsibilities in this battle. We will be looking at what our part is in ensuring Jesus' victory brings about the changes we desire in our lives. If we leave the Word of God as a theory, our lives will change very little and we will continue to struggle with the things that come against us even though Jesus has already defeated them. If however we understand from the Word of God what our part is and then act on it, we will start to move into the *experience* of what God wants us to have. He has paid the ultimate price for us to be free so let's not waste it by being complacent or ignorant of the truth[2]. Make a quality decision today to *'fight the good fight of faith'*[3] so that your testimony can be added to the countless millions of others regarding God's goodness and faithfulness.

"Father, thank You that victory over the enemy is already won. You've already done it Lord, and this victory is now mine because of my faith in You. I ask You Father to help me understand my responsibilities in this battle. Teach me what I need to do to appropriate Your victory into my own life, so that I can experience and then testify to Your goodness and strength in setting me free. I ask this in Jesus' Name. Amen."

Part 3

What is Our Responsibility?

'You Must Be Born Again'

"Do not be amazed that I said to you, 'You must be born again'."

(Jesus speaking to Nicodemus - John 3:7)

Unless we are born again, we cannot enter the Kingdom of God[1]. Unless we are born again we cannot understand spiritual things concerning God and His Word[2]. Being born again is a serious matter because without it we will remain in spiritual darkness[3] and will not be able to overcome the spiritual forces trying to destroy us.

Being born again means the old sinful nature we inherited from Adam is replaced with a brand new spirit that is from God[4]. It means we're adopted into God's family and become His sons and daughters[5]. The old nature cut us off from knowing God[6]; the new spiritual nature brings us into a close and personal relationship with Him so we can know Him as Father. It is no surprise therefore that Jesus said to Nicodemus *'you must be born again'*, with an emphasis I would imagine on the *must*.

There are ways we can know whether we are truly born again or not; one of them is to look at the 'fruit' we are producing. Is the fruit in our lives consistent with a new nature born of the Holy Spirit (love, joy, patience etc.); or are we still living in a way that is obviously sinful[7]? Fruit is always consistent with the source producing it (whether spiritual or physical), so what is our fruit saying regarding the nature within us[8]? We can't expect to be perfect, but is there enough evidence to convince us we have been born again of God's Spirit?

Jesus gives another indicator to help us know whether we are born again or not when He says *"He who is of God hears the words of God"*[9]. (The terms *'of God'*; *'born from above'* and *'born of the Spirit'* are synonymous with *'born again'*). Does God's Word speak to you when you read it? Is the Bible starting to make sense to you as you spend time in it? Growing in an understanding of the Word of God as we follow Jesus is a positive indicator of being born again, because the Holy Spirit is the One who gives us revelation of the Scriptures[10].

A further indicator of being born again is found in *1 John 5:1*, which tells us *'whoever believes that Jesus is the Christ is born of God'*. Believing in Jesus is more than mental assent. Believing in Jesus involves the heart - it's when an individual entrusts their spiritual well being to Christ. It means they recognise their salvation and eternal destiny is dependent on what Jesus has done for them, not what they're doing in an attempt to please God.

Where does this leave you? Hopefully the Holy Spirit will have given you the assurance that yes, you are born again. If you lack this assurance however then ask God for the gift of being born again without delay. You will then have the foundation to know Him as Father, He will adopt you into His family, and He will guide, lead, and strengthen you in the victories that lie ahead.

"Father, thank You for the gift of being born again. Thank You for drawing me to Yourself and adopting me into Your family. Thank You for giving me a sense of security, purpose, and worth in my life. Thank You that You are my faithful Father who will never leave me because my relationship with You is based on Your love for me, not on my performance. I live to know You Father so please would You draw me closer to You as I pray and read Your Word. In Jesus' Name I ask. Amen."

Day 19

Receive the Baptism of The Holy Spirit

"But you will receive power when the Holy Spirit has come upon you"

- Jesus (Acts 1:8)

The baptism of the Holy Spirit is offered to every follower of Jesus so they can be empowered to fulfil the ministry God has called them to here on earth. This includes the ministry in our own lives, in our families, our church, as well as in the world we live in. Even Jesus needed the baptism of the Holy Spirit. He was proclaimed God at His birth[1], yet He needed the baptism of the Holy Spirit before He could begin His supernatural ministry of healing, deliverance, and miracles[2]. Jesus hadn't performed any miracles until He had been baptised in the Holy Spirit.

The apostles we read about in the New Testament weren't mighty because of their own strength; they were mighty because they had been empowered by the Holy Spirit. Peter, a disciple of Jesus was overcome with fear the night before Jesus' crucifixion; even denying he was a follower of Jesus and cursing Him[3]. He was frightened that by associating himself with Jesus he would also be killed. Yet less than 2 months later Peter preached with boldness and confidence to thousands of people in Jerusalem, with about 3,000 of them putting their faith in Jesus[4]. That's because he and the other disciples had been filled with the Holy Spirit on the day of Pentecost[5].

In and of ourselves we cannot win the battle against fear, anxiety, and panic; or any other spiritual battle we may be engaged in. We don't have the power; neither do we have the strength to overcome. But once we are born again we have someone living inside us who *does* have the power, and who *does* have the strength[6]. His name is Jesus, and He's on our side. He wants us to win; He understands that without Him we can't win[7], which is why He is offering Himself to us in the Holy Spirit[8]. He wants us to fight in His strength, not our own. Will power, positive thinking, and self-discipline will not win this war - none of these can give us total freedom and victory. It's only by putting our faith and trust in *His* power and *His* victory that we become more than conquerors because His victory becomes ours[9].

The baptism of the Holy Spirit is not a gift we have to wrestle out of God's hands. He gives it freely and is waiting for us to receive it from Him by faith. He desires to give us the Holy Spirit because He loves us and because He is the perfect Father[10]. Our part is to recognise our need for the Holy Spirit in our lives, and then to come and ask Him with confidence and receive what we've asked for by faith[11]. If you haven't already done so, ask the Father today for the baptism of the Holy Spirit. Then believe you have received based on the truth that God is Good, and that He is Faithful.

"Father, it gives me great comfort to know I don't have to find the strength to win this battle in and of myself. Thank You that I don't have to depend on my own strength and ability because You are offering me Yours. I ask You for the gift You have promised, the baptism of the Holy Spirit so that I can be empowered not only to see victory in my own life, but for that victory to spill out into the lives of others also. I give You all the glory Lord, in the Name of Jesus. Amen."

Seek Wisdom and Get Understanding

"To start being wise you must first get wisdom.
No matter what it costs, get understanding."
Proverbs 4:7 (NIRV)

Wisdom is having the knowledge and understanding to make good choices and decisions that benefit the individual, their family, as well as other people. The Bible encourages us to seek God's wisdom above everything else[1] because it brings promotion, honour, protection, and favour[2]. A fool is simply someone who lacks wisdom[3], with the result they are unable to make good choices and decisions and so end up going from one problem to another[4]. If a fool were to seek wisdom, he would not remain a fool for long.

When my wife and I are in the car and we see someone driving recklessly we pray that God gives that person wisdom. Their reckless driving is a result of them not understanding what the consequences of their actions could lead to. The reality that they are endangering their own lives as well as the lives of others has not entered their minds, and even if it has they have not allowed it to make a difference so they remain foolish. Wisdom on the other hand would help them understand the dangers of what they are doing and would then equip them to make better choices.

None of us are exempt from foolishness however. We may not be foolish in our driving, but there are plenty of other areas in our lives that give us the opportunity to lack wisdom. I won't even begin to share with you some of the ways I have been foolish over the years - especially when I was young. God warns us in His Word that if we think we are wise and don't need to seek wisdom then we are actually worse than a fool ourselves![5]

Seeking the wisdom *that is from God* is the most important thing we can do because God's wisdom is perfect[6]. Man's wisdom does not even begin to compare with God's wisdom[7], yet in his foolishness and pride man rejects it[8]. Why would we not want to seek God's wisdom when His wisdom will give us the crown of life?[9]

Where can we find this precious wisdom of God? The answer is in the Lord Jesus Christ and His Word. God is offering us His Wisdom, and when we receive Jesus into our hearts God's wisdom comes as part of the package[10]. If we then go into the Word of God with a sincere humility, the Holy Spirit will reveal to us the will, thoughts, and intentions of God[11]. Humility on our part is essential though, because when we're humble we're acknowledging that we are seeking something we don't already possess[12]. Today, take time to humble yourself before God and confess that you continually need His wisdom. You will never regret it if you do, but there will certainly be times of regret if you don't.

"Father, I humble myself before You today and ask You to guide me and lead me in Your wisdom. I confess that often I think more highly of myself than I should do, for which I'm sorry Lord. Forgive me for the wrong choices, words, and decisions I've made in the past because I depended on my own wisdom, and I ask You Lord to stay close to me and prompt me with Your wisdom and counsel when You see me making a wrong choice. I ask this in Jesus' Name. Amen."

Day 21

Ask The Holy Spirit to Teach You

*"But when He, the Spirit of truth comes, He will
guide you into all the truth"*
John 16:13

The Bible tells us the 'knowledge of God' is held in a *'mystery'*[1]. What this means is that the truth about what God is really like (His nature, His will, His Kingdom etc.) is held in a realm *outside* of the natural intelligence and understanding of man[2]. The natural mind of a man cannot access this 'knowledge of God' no matter how hard it would try - because it is *spiritually appraised*[3].

The only way an individual can come into a true knowledge and understanding of God is by *revelation*. We can only come to know what God is *really* like - what His nature is, what His will is, what His desires are, by *revelation*. It has to be *revealed* to us because it is not something we can learn. That's why Jesus gave us His Holy Spirit[4]. It is the Holy Spirit who gives us 'access' into this true knowledge of God. The Holy Spirit knows the heart of God, so He is qualified and able to reveal to us the truth regarding God's nature and character[5].

Without the Holy Spirit an individual is carnal. Calling someone carnal is not an insult, it simply describes the individual who depends on their own intelligence, their own senses, and their own natural experiences to teach them whether something is true or not. Because the knowledge of God dwells in a realm outside of natural understanding[6], there is no way a carnal man or woman can access it so they will remain ignorant of the truth regarding what God's true nature is like[7]. They are then in danger of forming a distorted image of God based on their *natural* understanding, rather than a true understanding as *revealed* to them by the Holy Spirit.

Having the Holy Spirit reveal to us the truth about God is both a privilege and an honour. It is not something we should take for granted, nor should we miss the value of the gift we have been given[8]. It is essential for us to seize this privilege with both hands. If we want to truly know what God is like and the treasures He has in store for us then we have to be *intentional* in asking the Holy Spirit to reveal the truth of the Word of God to us. We have been given the Teacher who knows the heart, mind, and thoughts of God, and He wants to share those treasures with us[9]. But we need to ask Him; we need to make sure *He* knows we are looking to *Him* first and foremost to teach us the truth of God's Word. So make a commitment today that every time you read or study the Bible, you make a point of asking the Holy Spirit to teach you and reveal the truth to you. Acknowledge to Him that the truth you are seeking regarding God is outside of your own natural ability, and that you are looking to *Him* to reveal it to you. Then trust He will answer your prayer, because He will.

"Thank You Father for sending me the Holy Spirit to teach me the truth about You. I acknowledge Lord that I need Your Holy Spirit to reveal to me the truth contained in Your Word. I ask You Father to correct every wrong thinking I may have regarding what You are like - those things that have come as a result of past experiences, wrong teaching, or simple ignorance. I can't wait to get to know You better Lord through Your Word, and to find the genuine love and desire You have for me. In Jesus' Name I pray. Amen."

Pitch Your Tent in The Word of God

"If you continue in My word, then you are truly disciples of Mine; and you will know the truth, and the truth will make you free"
John 8:31-32

Jesus promises those who follow Him that if they *continue* in His Word they will come to know the truth and the truth will make them free[1]. The Greek word for *'continue'* carries a sense of dwelling somewhere. It means we are settled in a particular place and live there. That's what Jesus is telling us to do with His Word - He tells us to camp in it so that it becomes our home and our dwelling place. If we're prepared to take this attitude towards the Word of God then we will come to know the truth, and the truth will set us free.

It is only the truth *that we know* that sets us free. Truth can exist, but if we haven't come into the *knowledge* of it then it doesn't have the power to set us free. Consider the example of a man sitting outside the doctor's surgery waiting to go in for his test results. Understandably he is nervous because he picked up the concern in the doctor's voice at his last appointment. In the meantime the doctor is in his surgery and has checked the results - everything has come back normal. But the patient doesn't know this yet, so he is still anxious and is rehearsing the worst-case scenarios in his mind. The patient is free from illness, but because he hasn't come into the *knowledge* of this truth, he hasn't yet been set free from the fear and anxiety that he's currently experiencing. Once the doctor has shared the good news with him he will be relieved because he will have come into the truth for himself. The truth that he didn't have any illnesses already existed, but it wasn't until he came into the *knowledge* of that truth that he was set free.

It is the same with God's Word. There is truth within the Bible that has the potential to set us free in every area of our lives. It can set us free from sickness, guilt, shame, lack, bondage, oppression, in fact *anything* and *everything* we need to be set free from. God has designed it this way so we can experience His wholeness (*'shalowm'* - see Day 16). What Jesus is saying is that if we abide in His Word, if we're prepared to camp there then we will come into the knowledge of the truth it contains and be set free from the things oppressing us - whether spiritual or physical.

God is extremely confident about the truth of His Word and the freedom it can bring. He stands by it and promises that it will not fail - He even gives a guarantee it will work[2]. Who else other than God can say with such confidence and boldness that if we listen to what He says and then follow His commands we will find *'life'* and *'health to all our body'*?[3] The two most important decisions a person needs to make in their life is first of all to receive Jesus as Lord and Saviour, and then secondly to camp in His Word. In our journey to become free from the fear, panic, and anxiety that is attacking us, if we make a commitment to camp in God's Word there will only be one result - freedom[4].

"Thank You Father for giving me the Bible and that I have access to your promises. You have said Your Word is the key to my victorious life, and I believe You Lord. I ask You to help me make a commitment to seeking the truth contained in Your Word, and that You will give me the strength to remain consistently committed. Help me treasure Your Word Lord so that it becomes to me spiritual food that I cannot live without. I pray this in Jesus' Name. Amen."

Day 23

Use Your Spiritual Sword

"And take the helmet of salvation, and the sword of the Spirit,
which is the word of God"
Ephesians 6:17

The enemy of fear, panic, and anxiety cannot be 'seen' in the natural sense. Yet anyone who has experienced this type of oppression will testify to its existence as well as its reality. Because it is unseen, fighting it with natural weapons of warfare would be useless, so God has given us *spiritual* weapons to fight this *spiritual* enemy. What's more, these spiritual weapons are guaranteed to bring down even the strongest of enemies we may be facing[1].

One of these spiritual weapons is the *'sword of the Spirit, which is the Word of God'*[2]. The Greek word used for *'sword'* in this verse points to a short dagger-type sword no more than about 18 inches long (*'machaira'*). It was a particularly brutal weapon because it was razor sharp and used by Roman soldiers for close combat fighting. God wants us to see this as a picture of how we should use the Word of God as a weapon to inflict fatal damage on the spiritual enemy we are fighting.

The spirit of darkness will try to steal our health, our finances, our joy, our peace, our security, our relationships, in fact anything it can get its hands on[3]. Satan may try, but we're not defenceless because of the spiritual weapons God has given us. Not only can we defend ourselves with the Word of God, we can also go on the attack and drive the enemy back so that he eventually flees from us in terror[4]. The enemy is full of lies[5], so when we take up the 'sword of the Spirit' we are countering those lies with the truth of what God has said. The lies of the enemy cannot stand in the presence of the truth of what God has said, in the same way that darkness cannot stay in a room when the light is switched on.

The reason the Word of God is so powerful is because it carries the very Life of God within it[6]. It is God Himself that has spoken this Word[7], and when we speak the Word from a *heart of faith* then the Life of God contained within the Word is released into our situation. Declaring the Word of God over a particular situation should not be ritualistic; it needs to be done *in faith* because it is when it is done *in faith* that it becomes the *'sword of the Spirit'*. Our faith gives the Holy Spirit permission to use the Word on our behalf so that change can happen.

If you are not in the habit of declaring the Word of God over the situations you are facing, I would encourage you to start as soon as you can. Find some scriptures that apply to your situation and then start declaring them on a regular basis. It's not our declaring that brings about the change; it's the Life of God that is being released through our declaration of faith that brings the change. For those who are facing the enemy of fear, a good place to start would be with Deuteronomy 28:7; Isaiah 41:11-13 & 54:14-17; 2 Timothy 1:7; John 14:27; Hebrews 2:14-15; but don't limit yourself to these scriptures alone.

"Father, I can see myself holding a sword in my hand. This sword carries Your power and Your authority to destroy the enemy coming against me. This sword is Your Word. Thank You Lord for giving me this Sword, please teach me how to use it skilfully so that I will see the fear, panic, and anxiety fleeing from my life. In the Name of Jesus I ask. Amen."

Day 24

Speak To Your Mountain

"I tell you the truth, if you have faith and do not doubt, not only will you do what was done to the fig tree, but even if you say to this mountain, 'Be lifted up and thrown into the sea,' it will happen."

Jesus teaching His disciples - Matthew 21:21 (NET)

The Israelites were facing a huge challenge. The leader who had led them out of Egypt was now dead[1]. They were on the verge of crossing the river Jordan to enter the Promised Land but they knew they had a fight in front of them. Joshua was now their leader[2], so God gave him clear instructions regarding the way forward. One of the instructions He gave was *'this book of the law shall not depart from your mouth' (see Joshua 1:8)*

We would be foolish to ignore the instruction God gave Joshua, because tied to this instruction was the guarantee of success in the battles the Israelites would face[3]. In telling Joshua that the 'book of the law' (God's Word) should not depart from his *mouth*, He was instructing Joshua to speak the Word, to declare it, and to announce it. *It needed to come out of his mouth.* To the natural mind that can sound foolish, but if we want success in our battle against the *spiritual* forces that are opposing us, we need to use *spiritual* measures to deal with them. Speaking and declaring the Word of God is one of these spiritual measures. It needs to be done *in faith* however; not because our natural minds *understand* why we're doing it. We need do it because God is instructing us to; trusting that what God is commanding us to do is always right.

Jesus tells us words are *spiritual*, and that His words carry spiritual life[4]. Not all words carry spiritual life but His do, and ours can as well. Some words carry spiritual death, and the Bible tells us that whatever spiritual element the words of an individual carry (whether its life or death), the fruit in their lives will correspond to the spiritual component contained in the words they speak - whether life or death[5]. So if we're wise, we will speak the Word of God over our lives so that we will experience the fruit of the Life the Word contains.

Jesus tells us to speak to our problem (the 'mountain' that is facing us), and not to doubt. If we do, He promises the problem will eventually move out of our way[6]. Our natural mind will not understand how speaking to our 'mountain' will help, but if we trust Jesus and are faithful to what He is instructing us to do then we are walking *by faith*, not because our natural minds understand it[7]. The victory we will experience as a result of believing Jesus and acting by faith is unlimited[8].

If you are currently dealing with fear and anxiety, command it to leave in the Name of Jesus. Go to the scriptures where God promises to deliver you from your enemies and declare them and stand on them. The same principle applies to any problem you are facing - find God's promise regarding your situation and start speaking His Promise over your life and your family. As you do, you will be choosing the Life that God wants you to have, and it will eventually manifest[9].

"Thank You Father for giving me Your Word. Please give me a deeper revelation regarding the importance of declaring Your Word over my life and family, as well as the courage and boldness to speak to the 'mountains' I am facing. I trust You Lord. In Jesus' Name I pray. Amen."

Meditate On The Word of God

"I will meditate on all your works; I will ponder your deeds."

Psalm 77:12 (CEB)

God encourages us to meditate on His Word[1] but many Christians are hesitant. They are concerned it is somehow linked to the meditation that some Eastern religions practice. The meditation that is outside of the Word of God is potentially harmful because the individual is opening up their minds to things other than the truth of God's Word. Meditating on the Word of God however is to be encouraged because it is opening up the mind to what God is saying, and allowing God's truth to permeate our thinking and give direction to our lives.

Biblical meditation is not mysterious at all. Biblical meditation is simply taking a scripture or a verse, and then starting to 'chew' on it. The Hebrew word for 'meditate' in Psalm 77:12 (above) means *'to ponder, imagine, speak, study, talk, utter'*. Biblical meditation is setting ourselves some time to reflect on Scripture, allowing a verse to roll over in our minds, as well as speaking it out and asking ourselves questions such as *'do I really believe that?'*; or *'are You speaking to me Lord?'*. This is healthy meditation because it is giving the Holy Spirit the opportunity to speak to us through His Word so that the truth of the scripture is not limited to our minds, but is allowed to penetrate and sink into our hearts. It is a way of studying scripture that is *living* because the Holy Spirit will bring understanding and impress on us the truth the verse contains. The Holy Spirit is the anointing within us who knows all things, so if we ask Him, He will bring alive the scripture we're meditating on[2].

A victorious Christian has the Word of God *in their hearts,* not simply in their heads. It is with *the heart* a man believes[3], and it's out of the heart that words come[4]. So if we want to speak faith-filled words that remove the 'mountains' in our lives then we need to get faith into our hearts in the first instance! It is by pondering on, contemplating, and uttering the Word of God during our times of meditation that faith gets down into our hearts[5] which then means we can speak words of faith that bring victory.

Spend time in the Scriptures and ask the Holy Spirit to speak to you personally through a verse or a passage as you read. When a verse comes alive for you, don't go any further. Stay on that verse and start speaking it to yourself, reflect on it, asking the Holy Spirit to take you deeper. Personalise the verse and allow the truth it contains to drop into your heart, and if necessary go back to the same verse/s again and again. Most importantly, enjoy the privilege of having the One who created you speak to you personally!

"Father, please teach me how to meditate on Your Word. I long to hear Your sweet, gentle voice speak to me. Help me set time aside so I can learn how to hear Your voice. Thank You once again that Your plans and thoughts towards me are to prosper me, and to do good for me. In Jesus' Name I thank You. Amen."

Day 26

Look Beyond What You Can See

"For we walk by faith, not by sight"
2 Corinthians 5:7

We can be faced with situations in our lives that look impossible to overcome. What our eyes are showing us, what other people are saying to us, and what our past experiences have taught us can tell us we are in a hopeless situation and facing defeat. Everything is pointing that way it seems, except the Word of God. When everything in the natural is telling us there is no hope of victory, we need to know what God says about our situation, and then put our trust in Him.

That's what Abraham did. God promised Abraham he would be *'a father of many nations'*[1], yet at the age of about a hundred years old he was still without an heir[2]. *Everything* in the natural pointed to failure. Even though the facts and circumstances were offering him no hope, he had a hope within him that was born out of God's promise that he and Sarah would have a son[3]. Abraham took the hope he had been given by God through a promise, and countered the hopelessness of what his natural circumstances told him[4].

Abraham did not allow his natural understanding, his natural senses, or his circumstances to dictate to him what he believed. Despite *everything* in the natural pointing towards defeat, he continued to believe and trust God's promise and as he did he *'grew strong in faith'*[5]. He became *'fully assured'* that the promise God had given him and Sarah would come to pass[6]. Isaac's birth was the result of Abraham and Sarah's faith - they wholeheartedly trusted God's promise to them (His Word), not what circumstances were telling them[7].

Faith is the power that will overcome *every* challenge we face so that we come through victorious[8]. Faith is looking beyond what our natural senses are telling us and putting our trust and hope ONLY in what God has promised us in His Word. Faith is being so absorbed with the promise of God for our situation that it starts to make us 'blind' to what our senses and circumstances are trying to tell us. We're not denying the facts; we're simply denying their right to determine what we believe and Who we trust.

Faith sees first and foremost what God has said about our situation (from His Word), and is so focused on God's promise that we start getting 'tunnel vision'. We're aware of the negative circumstances and facts that tell us things look impossible, but we're so focused on what God has said that we see right through them into the Promise, which lies beyond the circumstances.

Are you facing something that seems impossible? There is no need to deny the facts, but put all your effort into what God has said regarding your situation. Then make a decision to believe *Him*, not what facts are saying, and then stay on it. Take this opportunity to grow in the inner man just like Abraham did - there is no reason we can't because our faith is exactly the same as the faith that brought Abraham victory[9].

"Father, I thank You so much that facts and circumstances don't have the 'final word' regarding my life. You have the final Word, and Your Word is always hopeful even in the most impossible of situations. Show me Father what You have said about my situation, and help me to put my hope and trust fully in what You have said, knowing You are Faithful. Thank You Lord, in Jesus' Name I pray. Amen."

Renew Your Mind

"Don't be conformed to this world, but be transformed by the renewing of your mind, so that you may prove what is the good, well-pleasing, and perfect will of God."
Romans 12:2 (World English Bible)

One of the greatest dangers facing the born-again Christian is a failure to renew their mind. Christ comes to live within us when we are the born-again[1], yet there is little or no opportunity for Him to make a difference in our lives unless we renew our mind.

When a person is born-again their spirit becomes brand new[2] but their soul remains unchanged (soul = mind + will + emotions). Even though Christ dwells *in their spirit*, they will continue to think, speak, and behave in the same way they did before being saved unless they allow their mind to be renewed by the Spirit of God. Renewal of the mind simply means replacing the old carnal way of thinking, behaving, and speaking (that existed before being saved); with God's way of thinking, speaking, and behaving which He shares freely with us in His Word. It is as we renew our minds that the Christ within us is released and we then begin to see victory in our lives.

Renewal of the mind is not automatic - it has to be intentional, and it is a lifelong process. The main (and foundational) way of renewing our minds is through the Word of God. Surrendering to the leading, counsel, and teaching of the Holy Spirit as we study the Word will bring us into the knowledge and understanding of God's truth (see Day 21). As we begin to understand this revealed truth and then act on it, we will see our limited, natural, and often destructive ways of thinking being replaced by the life-giving, supernatural, and excellent thoughts of God[3].

Another important element in renewing our minds is to pray in tongues *and then ask God for interpretation*. When we are born-again we are given the Holy Spirit[4]. In receiving the Holy Spirit, *'the anointing that knows all things'*[5] and *'the mind of Christ'*[6] is deposited within us. Praying in the Spirit releases this *'anointing that knows all things'* and *'the mind of Christ'*; which means when we pray in the Spirit we are uttering the 'mysteries' (the hidden truths) about the Kingdom of God[7]. If we then ask God for interpretation as Paul instructs us to do[8], the Holy Spirit will help us understand *with our natural mind* those things which are *spiritually appraised*[9]. Praying in tongues and then asking God for interpretation means that the hidden spiritual truths about God and His Kingdom are deposited into our natural understanding by the Holy Spirit.

Take full advantage of the gift of Christ within you by making sure you are on the path of having your mind renewed by the Holy Spirit. Make the Word of God foundational in your life and if you have not received the gift of praying in tongues, then ask God for it. If you are not sure how to go about things, share with a trusted Christian and ask them to pray with you to receive the gift. God gives good gifts to His children[10], so make sure you don't lose out on the gifts He is offering you.

"Thank You Father that You want me to grow in You. Thank You for the gift of the Holy Spirit and help me to surrender to Him fully so that I can renew my mind and become the person You have designed me to be. Take my life Lord and please make a difference with it. In Jesus' Name I pray. Amen."

Resist the Devil, Stand Firm, and Be Patient

"Submit yourselves to God: resist the devil, and he will flee from you."

James 4:7 (GNV)

When we experience fear, panic, or anxiety, it's important to understand they are not from God. God has not given us a spirit of fear[1] - in fact He has done the complete opposite because He has given us His Peace[2]. Fear and panic bring confusion, so fear is clearly not from God because He is 'not the author of confusion'[3]. Understanding these truths *mentally* is one thing, but its as we journey with God that we come to know it *in our hearts*. As we come to know His nature and character, we will come to recognise He is the Perfect loving Father who gives good gifts to His children, not destructive ones.

The devil is behind fear, panic, and anxiety, as well as every other destructive force that tries to destroy us[4]. Once we recognise this truth we need to start resisting him. We need to stand up against the devil and refuse to accept the fear he is bringing. We are not meant to resist in our own strength and in our own authority, but rather in the strength and authority of the One who has already defeated the enemy we are resisting. Our faith in Jesus means His victory becomes ours, and it is in Jesus' victory over the devil that we stand. When we do that, the devil is left with no option other then to flee from us because he knows he will not be able to defeat us[5].

Jesus has shown us how to resist the devil. When the devil came against Jesus in the wilderness, He used the Word of God to resist the devil's temptations[6]. Every time the devil tried to get Jesus to submit to his temptation, Jesus came back at the devil with *'It is written'*, and then quoted Scripture. This is what we need to do also, which is why it's essential for us to know the Scripture promises regarding our situation. It is as we speak the truth of what God has said over our lives that the devil has to flee because God's truth always triumphs over the devil's lies.

It would be wonderful to see the devil flee from us the very first time we speak the truth of God's Word against his lies, but that's not always what happens. Often we have to take a *continual* stand regarding an issue - it's as if the devil is trying to gauge how serious we are in resisting him and how much value we actually place on God's Word. It can sometimes feel as if we're not making any progress at all, but if we look back at where we started we will definitely be encouraged because we'll see the progress we're making.

Do you need to make a stand against the devil in any area of your life? When you make your stand <u>keep your focus on the Word of God</u>, not the devil. Keep the promises of God before you and get them down into your heart. Make a decision to stand for as long as it takes to see it through. It is the Christian who refuses to quit because they wholeheartedly trust God's Promise (in His Word) that see breakthroughs in their lives. Make every effort to be one of them.

"Father, thank You that I'm not facing this enemy in my own strength, but in Yours. Help me to take the step of faith to resist the enemy that is trying to steal from me. Thank You Lord that You have already won this battle; so please help me to remember the devil is already defeated and so has no option but to flee from me. In Jesus' Name I pray. Amen."

Day 29

Guard Your Heart!

"Guard your heart more than anything else, because the source
of your life flows from it."
Proverbs 4:23 (GW)

Think for a moment about the protection that is afforded the
President of the United States. The huge team of bodyguards
and the bombproof Cadillac are just the tip of the iceberg. I
sense from Proverbs 4:23 (above) that God is telling us that
from a spiritual perspective; we should be giving our hearts the
same level of protection.

When the Bible talks about the 'heart' it is not referring to the
physical organ that pumps blood round the body - it is
referring to the spiritual seat of government within us. Our
heart is the very centre of who we are and it's where we make
our decisions and choices.

We should be fervently guarding our hearts because our life
flows from it. In other words, whatever comes out of our hearts
determines the sort of life we have. This is what Proverbs 4:23
is telling us! Jesus tells us the mouth speaks out of the
abundance of the heart, so whatever a person has in their hearts
(whether good or evil) will be revealed by their words[1]. In
addition, James tells us that words control the direction of a
person's life - he compares the tongue to a bit in a horse's
mouth, as well as a 'rudder' governing the direction of a ship[2].
So whatever is in a person's heart comes out in their words, and those
words then determine the direction of their life. This is a very
serious situation.

The good news is we can choose what words come out of our mouths simply by choosing what goes into our hearts in the first instance. Our spiritual heart is like a water tank that constantly needs to be topped up. We are the ones tasked with the responsibility of what sort of water goes in - either clean or dirty - it's our choice. The three main 'entry points' by which we fill this tank are the eyes, the ears, and the mouth. These are the 'portals' of entry into our hearts. The things we look at, listen to, and speak about are what fill our spiritual heart, so if we are exposing ourselves to fear and anxiety through films, music, and books etc. then fear is what will fill our heart. The words we then speak out of the overflow[3] will reflect what we've put in, which in turn will take us in a direction we don't want to go[4]. On the other hand if we give attention to God's Word and listen to what He says (Bible / CD / DVD teaching etc.), we will be filling our heart with the Life that His Word contains[5]. Our words will then have *His* Life within them, and will take us in the direction of the abundant life He has for us[6].

The bottom line is that we are able to influence the direction of our lives. If we want to follow God's plan for our lives then we need to fill our hearts with His Life. As we look into God's Word and start speaking His promises, we will be guided towards the health, the security, the peace, and the joy He desires for us to have. Today, ask the Holy Spirit to give you wisdom to know how to guard your heart, and then make a declaration that you are choosing His direction for your life.

'Father, I ask You to help me see how important the words I speak are. Help me to fill the tank of my heart with the clean water of Your Word. Help me take care with the words I speak, and please tell me when I'm speaking words that do not agree with what You have planned for me so I can be corrected. I ask You this in Jesus' Name. Amen."

Day 30

Use The Name of Jesus!

*"So God lifted him up to the highest place. God gave him
the name that is above every name."*

Philippians 2:9 (NIRV)

There is a spiritual enemy out to destroy us[1], and his name is
satan. Even though satan is a threat, the Christian does not
need to fear him because Jesus has already defeated him on our
behalf. When our faith is in Jesus Christ we are positioned in a
place of total and complete victory over our adversary. That's
because the victory of the One who has crushed him becomes
ours - simply as a result of putting our faith in Jesus[2].

The name of Jesus is not a 'lucky charm' to add onto the end of
our prayers. From a spiritual perspective, the Name of Jesus is
like the most powerful nuclear missile known to man, a
weapon no enemy can hope to match. When we pray, ask, or
speak in the Name of Jesus it means *we are speaking from a
position of possessing all the attributes that name brings*. So when
we use the Name of Jesus, it means we are positioned in a *place
of victory, a place of authority, and a place of power*. This is the
result of God placing us 'in Christ' when we put our faith in
Jesus, and then giving us His Name so we could rule and reign
with Him[3].

Jesus was perfectly righteous, so when He prayed the Father
always heard Him[4]. When *we* come to the Father and ask in the
Name of Jesus[5], God will hear our prayers because we also are
righteous. We are not righteous through our own actions or

deeds, but righteous because of our faith in Christ[6]. Asking in the Name of Jesus means we are clothing ourselves with Christ's perfect righteousness, so we're able to come boldly before Him, confident of seeing our prayers answered[7].

Having the Name of Jesus also means we can speak with *His authority*. Jesus promises us that if we speak to our mountains (the problems we face), they will move[8]. When we speak to the mountain in the Name of Jesus, we are speaking from a position of having all the attributes the Name of Jesus brings - which includes His authority. But we must speak *in faith and not doubt*. We need to believe that the Name of Jesus carries all authority, and then believe that our mountain will move as a result of His Name. Heaven's resources are available to us in the same way they were for Jesus[9], because we've been given His Name.

The Name of Jesus has authority over every other name. *Everything* has to subject itself to the Name of Jesus[10]. It doesn't matter whether it is physical, emotional, or spiritual - any and every problem we may face has to bow to the authority that the Name of Jesus carries. If you are currently dealing with fear, panic, or anxiety, then command it to leave in the Name of Jesus. Put your faith in the authority of His Name and stand your ground for as long as it takes. The Name of Jesus is the Name above every name so it will only be a matter of time before your mountain has to move[11].

"Father, thank You that You have given me Your Name. Your Name Jesus is above every name, which means everything has to subject itself to Your Name. Take me into a deeper understanding Lord of what it means to have Your Name; not only so I can see mountains moved in my own life, but also in the lives of other people. Let it all be for Your glory Lord. I ask this in Your Precious Name. Amen."

Endnotes

(Scriptural references)

Endnotes

Day 1

1. Ephesians 6:12
2. Genesis 46:6-7
3. Exodus 1:8-10
4. Exodus 1:11-14
5. Exodus 5:6-11
6. Exodus 5:14; 16
7. Exodus 3:7

Day 2

1. Exodus 7-12
2. Exodus 14:5-7
3. Exodus 14:9-10
4. Exodus 14:21-22
5. Exodus 14:23
6. Exodus 14:25
7. Exodus 14:28

Day 3

1. Exodus 15:22-23
2. Exodus 15:25

Day 4

1. Exodus 15:22-27
2. Exodus 15:26
3. Hebrews 13:8

Day 5

1. Deuteronomy 8:7-9
2. Exodus 13:17-18
3. Exodus 23:23; Deuteronomy 1:30, 3:22, 9:3, 11:23, 31:3; Joshua 10:8 & 42, 23:3
4. Numbers 33:53
5. Deuteronomy 7:22
6. Deuteronomy 11:22-25
7. Numbers 33:50-52; 55
8. Hebrews 4:1-11
9. Romans 8:37
10. 1 Timothy 6:12

Endnotes

Day 6

1. Joshua 2:8-11
2. Joshua 2:23-24
3. Joshua 2:11
4. Romans 8:37-39
5. James 4:7

Day 7

1. John 4:24
2. Matthew 1:23
3. Isaiah 43:11, 45:21-22; Hosea 13:4
4. Luke 2:11
5. Matthew 5:17
6. John 1:1-2
7. John 1:14
8. 2 Corinthians 1:20
9. Hebrews 2:14-15
10. Galatians 5:1
11. John 6:28-29

Day 8

1. Matthew 20:28; Mark 10:45
2. Acts 4:12
3. Romans 6:16
4. Jeremiah 29:11
5. Isaiah 53:5
6. John 10:10

Day 9

1. John 8:34; Romans 6:16
2. Matthew 28:18; Philippians 2:9-11
3. Luke 11:20
4. John 5:24; Colossians 1:13
5. John 5:24; 10:10
6. Galatians 5:1

Day 10

1. Matthew 9:20-22; Mark 6:56 *as examples*
2. Matthew 8:16; Luke 8:26-36 *as examples*
3. Matthew 14:13-21; 15:32-38
4. John 8:2-11
5. Hebrews 13:8
6. John 19:30

Day 11

1. Ephesians 6:12
2. Romans 8:15; 2 Timothy 1:7
3. John 8:44
4. John 1:17; 14:6
5. John 17:17
6. James 4:7

Day 12

1. Hebrews 2:14
2. 1 John 2:2
3. Isaiah 53:4-5, 10; Galatians 5:1
4. Romans 5:8
5. 2 Corinthians 5:21
6. Isaiah 52:14
7. Isaiah 53:4
8. 1 Corinthians 6:19
9. Romans 8:2

Day 14

1. Matthew 26:3-4; Luke 22:1-2; John 5:18
2. Colossians 1:15
3. Hebrews 1:3
4. John 5:19
5. John 8:28
6. Hebrews 2:14
7. John 1:14
8. Mark 1:40-41; Luke 4:40
9. Matthew 9:36; 14:14; Mark 6:34; 8:2. The Greek word translated 'compassion' (*'splagchnizomai'*) literally means *'to have the bowels yearn'*.
10. John 6:38
11. Jeremiah 31:31 & 34; John 1:12-13
12. John 17:26, 20:17

Endnotes

Day 15

[1] Genesis 1:26; Psalm 8:4-8
[2] Genesis 2:16-17
[3] Romans 6:16
[4] Romans 11:29
[5] Psalm 51:5; Romans 5:12
[6] John 3:3-8
[7] Luke 1:35
[8] John 10:17-18
[9] Matthew 28:18-19; Matthew 10:1, 16:19; Mark 16:14-18
[10] Deuteronomy 28:13; Matthew 5:17; 2 Corinthians 1:20

Day 16

[1] Hosea 1:7; Zephaniah 3:17-19; Zechariah 8:7&13; 9:9&16; 10:6
[2] Luke 2:11
[3] Matthew 9:20-22; Mark 6:56 as examples
[4] Luke 8:26-36 as an example
[5] John 8:10-11
[6] Matthew 27:26; Isaiah 50:6
[7] Matthew 26:67; 27:30; John 18:22; Isaiah 50:6
[8] Acts 2:22-23

Day 17

[1] The Greek word is *'katargeo'*
[2] Hosea 4:6
[3] 1 Timothy 6:12

Day 18

[1] John 3:5
[2] John 3:3, 8:47; 1 Corinthians 2:14
[3] John 12:35 & 46
[4] 2 Corinthians 5:17; 1 John 5:1
[5] John 1:12-13; Romans 8:15
[6] Isaiah 59:2; Romans 8:6-7
[7] Galatians 5:16-25
[8] Matthew 7:16-18
[9] John 8:47
[10] John 16:13; 1 Corinthians 2:9-12

Endnotes

Day 19

1. Luke 2:11
2. Luke 4:14; Matthew 4:23-25
3. Matthew 26:69-75
4. Acts 2:14-41
5. Acts 2:1-4
6. John 14:16-17
7. John 15:5
8. John 14:18-20
9. Romans 8:37
10. Luke 11:9-13; 12:32
11. 1 John 5:14-15; Hebrews 11:6; James 1:6

Day 20

1. Proverbs 3:13-15; 16:16
2. Proverbs 3:35; 4:6-9; 14:3; 14:35
3. Proverbs 1:7; 10:21; 18:2; 23:9; 24:7; 28:26
4. Proverbs 1:32; 10:14; 10:21; 13:16; 14:16; 18:7; 26:11
5. Proverbs 26:12
6. James 3:17
7. 1 Corinthians 1:25
8. Proverbs 1:20-32; John 1:9-11; 1 Corinthians 1:18
9. Proverbs 4:9; 14:18
10. 1 Corinthians 1:30
11. John 16:13; 1 Corinthians 2:9-12
12. James 1:5; 4:6

Day 21

1. Mark 4:11; Ephesians 1:9, 3:4, 6:19
2. 1 Corinthians 2:6-8
3. 1 Corinthians 2:14
4. John 16:12-15
5. 1 Corinthians 2:10-11
6. Isaiah 55:8-9
7. 1 Corinthians 2:11
8. Matthew 13:16-17
9. 1 Corinthians 2:9-12; Psalm 51:6

Endnotes

Day 22

1. John 8:31-32
2. Psalm 138:2; Isaiah 55:10-11; Matthew 7:24-27
3. Proverbs 4:20-22
4. Galatians 5:1; James 1:25

Day 23

1. 2 Corinthians 10:3-5
2. Ephesians 6:17
3. John 10:10
4. Deuteronomy 28:7; James 4:7
5. John 8:44
6. Hebrews 4:12
7. 2 Timothy 3:16

Day 24

1. Deuteronomy 34:5-8
2. Deuteronomy 31:23, 34:9; Joshua 1:1-2
3. Joshua 1:8
4. John 6:63
5. Proverbs 18:21
6. Matthew 21:21; Mark 11:23
7. Proverbs 3:5; 2 Corinthians 5:7
8. 1 John 5:4; Mark 9:23
9. Deuteronomy 30:19-20; Jeremiah 29:11; James 3:4-5

Day 25

1. Psalm 1:2; 119:15 & 27; 145:5
2. 1 John 2:27
3. Romans 10:10
4. Matthew 12:34b-35
5. Romans 10:17

Endnotes

Day 26

[1.] Genesis 15:4-6; Romans 4:17
[2.] Romans 4:19
[3.] Genesis 18:10-14
[4.] Romans 4:18
[5.] Romans 4:20
[6.] Romans 4:21
[7.] Hebrews 11:11-12
[8.] 1 John 5:4
[9.] Galatians 3:7, 9

Day 27

[1.] Galatians 2:20; Colossians 1:27
[2.] 2 Corinthians 5:17
[3.] Isaiah 55:8-9; 1 Corinthians 2:9-13
[4.] Romans 5:5; 1 Corinthians 2:12, 6:19; Galatians 4:6
[5.] 1 John 2:27
[6.] 1 Corinthians 2:16
[7.] 1 Corinthians 14:2
[8.] 1 Corinthians 14:13
[9.] 1 Corinthians 2:12-14
[10.] Luke 11:13; James 1:17

Day 28

[1.] 2 Timothy 1:7; Romans 8:15
[2.] John 14:27
[3.] 1 Corinthians 14:33
[4.] John 10:10
[5.] 1 John 4:4; 5:18
[6.] Matthew 4:1-11

Day 29

[1.] Matthew 12:34-35
[2.] James 3:4-5
[3.] Matthew 12:34
[4.] James 3:4-5
[5.] Hebrews 4:12
[6.] Jeremiah 29:11; Proverbs 4:20-23

Day 30

[1] John 8:44, 10:10 & 17:15; 1 Peter 5:8
[2] Romans 8:37
[3] Romans 5:17; Ephesians 2:5-6
[4] John 11:41-42
[5] John 16:23
[6] Romans 3:21-22
[7] Hebrews 4:16; 10:22; 1 John 5:14-15
[8] Mark 11:23
[9] Matthew 26:53
[10] Philippians 2:9-10
[11] Matthew 21:21-22